MIGHTY ANIMAL MIGRATIONS

A MONARCH BUTTERFLY'S JOURNEY

David and Julie Lavender

Enslow PUBLISHING

Please visit our website, www.enslow.com. For a free color catalog of all our high-quality books, call toll free 1-800-398-2504 or fax 1-877-980-4454

Published in 2027 by
Enslow Publishing
2544 Clinton Street
Buffalo, NY 14224

Cataloging-in-Publication Data
Names: Lavender, David R., 1961-, author. | Lavender, Julie, author.
Title: A monarch butterfly's journey / by David and Julie Lavender.
Description: Buffalo, NY : Enslow Publishing, 2027. | Series: Mighty animal migrations | Includes glossary.
Identifiers: ISBN 9781978549548 (pbk.) | ISBN 9781978549555 (library bound) | ISBN 9781978549562 (ebook)
Subjects: LCSH: Monarch butterfly--Migration--Juvenile literature.
Classification: LCC QL561.D3 L384 2027 | DDC 595.7891568--dc23

Photo credits: Cover, p 1, Danita Delimont/Shutterstock.com; Calendars used throught interior, Evolvect/AdobeStock.com; p 4, Butterfly Hunter/Shutterstock.com; p 5, Diane Woodcheke/Shutterstock.com; p 6, Brian Donovan/Shutterstock.com; p 7, Nandalal Sarkar/Shutterstock.com; p 8, Leena Robinson/Shutterstock.com; p 9, Manuel Balesteri/Shutterstock.com; p 10, Melola/Shutterstock.com; p 11, Sari ONeal/Shutterstock.com, AMR Captures/Shutterstock.com; p 12, Naeemphotographer2/Shutterstock.com; p 13, JHVEPhoto/Shutterstock.com; p 14, John Benedict Malong/Shutterstock.com; p 15, Isabelle OHara/Shutterstock.com; p 16, 1000Photography/Shutterstock.com; p 17, GreyBeard22/Shutterstock.com; p 18, Ana Sha/Shutterstock.com; p 19, alexutulescu/Shutterstock.com; p 20, Sari ONeal/Shutterstock.com; p 21, Antho B, Maryunin Yury Vasilevich/Shutterstock.com; p 22, Linda McKusick/Shutterstock.com; p 23, Bob Hilscher/Shutterstock.com; p 24, Butterfly Hunter/Shutterstock.com; p 25, Kim Howell/Shutterstock.com; p 26, Bob Hilscher/Shutterstock.com; p 27, javarman/Shutterstock.com; p 29, AI generated

Printed in China

CPSIA compliance information: Batch #QSENS27: For further information, contact Enslow Publishing, New York, New York, at 1-800-398-2504.

Table of Contents

Mystery Migration

Millions of animals migrate each year. They travel by land, sea, or air. They push forward in search of food or better weather conditions. Or to find a mate. Or maybe to find a better place to give birth.

Every year, millions of monarch butterflies fly south for the winter. They can't survive the cold winters in the north. They fly from many places in North America to the same forest in Mexico.

Scientists can't explain how the monarchs know just exactly where to go. It's a mystery!

Monarch Moments

Monarchs that travel the farthest come from the southern parts of Ontario and Quebec. The longest monarch journey from Canada to Mexico is almost 3,000 miles (4,800 km). That's a long trip for an animal that weighs less than a paper clip!

An Egg Hatches

One sunny August morning in Quebec, Canada, a tiny monarch caterpillar pushes her way out of an egg. The egg is stuck to a leaf on a milkweed plant.

First, she eats her eggshell. Next, she munches on the thin hairs on the bottom of the milkweed leaf. Then, she gobbles the milkweed leaf with lots of tiny bites.

She eats and eats, almost all day long. She stops eating to shed her skin when she outgrows it. Then, she eats more. The caterpillar keeps growing bigger. She will shed her skin four times.

Newly hatched monarch caterpillar larva eating the egg from which it emerged.

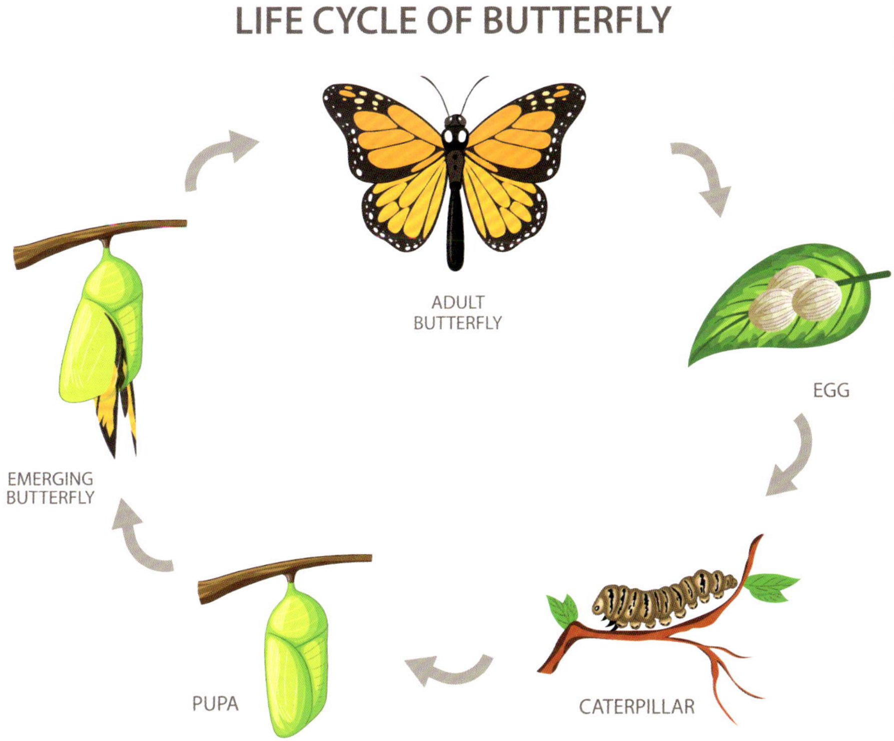

Monarch Moments

Insects like monarch butterflies go through a growth process called **metamorphosis**. That means they change completely as they go through each life stage. The four parts of a monarch's metamorphosis are: egg, larva, pupa, and adult. The caterpillar is the larva stage.

Big Changes

The caterpillar eats for 14 days. Then, she crawls off the plant. She climbs a nearby shrub. She needs a safe location for the next change.

The caterpillar forms a silk mat on a small stem. She pushes silk from the **spinneret** on the bottom of her head to make the sticky mat. Then, she presses her back legs into the silk and hangs upside down in a "J" shape.

She sheds her skin one more time. Her green **chrysalis** shows now. The cells inside her body make big changes.

Monarch Moments

The chrysalis stage is also called the pupa. During this stage, wings form and adult organs develop.

Time to Migrate

Fifteen days later, something incredible happens. The chrysalis begins to split. An orange and black butterfly emerges!

The monarch butterfly pumps fluid into her wings to unfold them. It takes several hours for the wings to dry.

She flaps her wings once. Then again. Once more, and her wings are ready. It's time to migrate!

Viceroy butterfly

Monarch butterfly

Monarch Moments

Milkweed is toxic to some animals. Most birds won't eat monarchs because of the milkweed poison. Viceroy butterflies **mimic** monarchs so birds won't eat them either.

Super Butterfly!

The new monarch is part of the "super **generation**" of monarchs. Scientists call them "super" because they'll live up to nine months. Other generations of monarchs only live two to four weeks.

She leaves Quebec and flies south. Monarchs fly to the same place each year. This young butterfly is headed to the mountains of Central Mexico.

Monarch Moments

Shorter days and cooler temperatures tell a monarch when it's time to migrate south.

A Long Journey

The new monarch flaps her wings. She has a long way to go. She sometimes flies higher to catch a better wind. She rests and sips on nectar along the way. This gives her the energy she needs.

At night, she'll roost in a pine tree. Most of the time, she rests in a tree with other monarchs. They're on their way to Mexico too.

Week after week, she flies. Finally, she reaches the Sierra Madre mountains. She lands on the branch of an oyamel fir tree. Millions of monarch butterflies have already arrived. She'll **overwinter** here.

« Sierra Madre mountains

Monarch Moments

When they get to Mexico, monarchs gather in trees to stay warm. The weight of so many butterflies clustered together can sometimes cause a branch to break!

Western Monarchs

Monarch butterflies that live west of the Rocky Mountains do not migrate to Mexico. They migrate to the California coast instead.

Once they get to California, they roost for the winter in eucalyptus trees, cypress trees, and pine trees.

Western monarchs, like eastern monarchs, use **instinct** to find their way during migration. They use cues from the sun and Earth's **magnetic field** to guide their journey.

Monarch butterflies cluster in eucalyptus trees.

Monarch Moments

Monarchs that live in southern Florida do not migrate at all. Warmer temperatures and plenty of milkweed plants throughout the winter allow them to stay there all year long.

Winter Is Over

When winter ends, the female monarch leaves Mexico. She flies north until she reaches Texas.

She mates, then begins her search for milkweed plants. She flaps and flies until she finds just the right plant.

She lays an egg on a milkweed leaf. She leaves a bit of liquid there too. It acts like glue and helps the egg stick to the leaf and not fall off.

Monarch butterfly laying an egg on milkweed leaf.

Monarch Moments

Monarchs don't eat much while they overwinter, but they do need water. The fog and clouds provide moisture. Tall trees in the mountains protect them from wind and bad weather, like snow or rain.

A New Generation

The female monarch flits from milkweed to milkweed, leaving eggs each time she lands. She drinks nectar from a pink flower nearby. Then, she searches for more milkweed.

She lays about 500 eggs. Soon, her "super" butterfly job is over. She lived for nine months, but a new generation will take over next.

After four days, a tiny monarch caterpillar pushes her way out of the egg. The cycle begins again. Caterpillar, chrysalis, butterfly. Scientists call them Generation One because they are the first monarchs of the year.

A monarch egg on a milkweed leaf is about to hatch.

Monarch Moments

The monarch's journey comes with problems. Ants, spiders, and wasps attack monarch caterpillars. Some birds eat monarch butterflies, even though most birds avoid the milkweed toxins. Bad weather conditions can damage butterfly wings or cause their death.

Must Keep Migrating

The new butterfly mates and lays eggs. Then, she takes flight and migrates north, drinking nectar and laying eggs along the way.

When she gets to Tennessee, her lifespan is almost over. She lays more eggs, and those butterflies become the second generation.

A second-generation butterfly continues the migration. She stops along the way to find nectar and lay eggs. She makes it all the way to Pennsylvania.

Monarch Moments

Each generation of monarch travels further north. It will take four generations to make it back to Canada.

Moving Farther North

Butterflies that emerge in Pennsylvania are part of the third generation of monarchs. A new butterfly mates and continues the journey. The story sounds the same—egg, caterpillar, chrysalis, butterfly.

The new butterfly flies all the way to Quebec. And, you guessed it! She finds milkweed plants and lays eggs. Egg, caterpillar, chrysalis, butterfly.

The fourth monarch generation emerges. The butterfly will not mate or lay eggs now. The fourth generation is the "super generation." Her job is to fly south, all the way to Mexico. It's time for a new migration.

JULY
AUGUST

More than One Generation

Monarch migrations are unusual. It takes more than one generation of butterflies to complete the whole cycle. At least four generations take part in a monarch migration.

Yet every year, monarchs take flight in a remarkable migration. How do monarchs know how to get to the Sierra Madre mountains in Mexico? Not even scientists can answer that question. It's part of the monarch migration mystery.

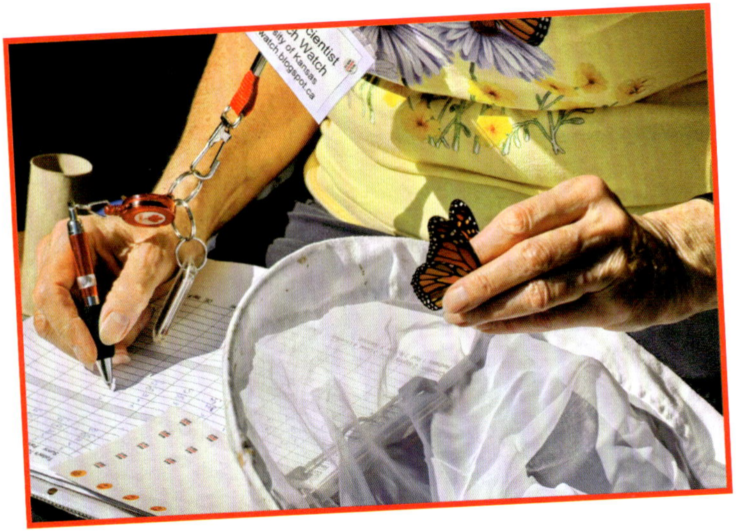

A scientist tags a monarch butterfly to track its migration.

Monarch Moments

Migrating monarchs usually fly between 50 and 100 miles (80 and 161 km) a day. The migration south can take two months. The longest recorded monarch journey was 265 miles in one day!

A Monarch Migration Map

1. The "super generation" of monarchs that live east of the Rocky Mountains begin their migration south to Mexico. This takes place in autumn.
2. Monarchs that live west of the Rocky Mountains begin their migration to California for the winter. They leave in fall too. In the spring, they'll fly away from California, heading to their summer breeding locations west of the Rocky Mountains.
3. The monarch butterflies overwinter in the Sierra Madre mountains in Mexico.
4. In spring, monarchs make their way north again. It will take several generations of butterflies to complete the entire migration.
5. The next generation of monarchs continue the journey north.
6. Another generation hatches and continues north.
7. One more generation of monarch butterflies takes part in the great migration.
8. The monarch butterfly has completed the journey. Soon, it will be time for the next "super generation" of monarch butterflies to head south again.

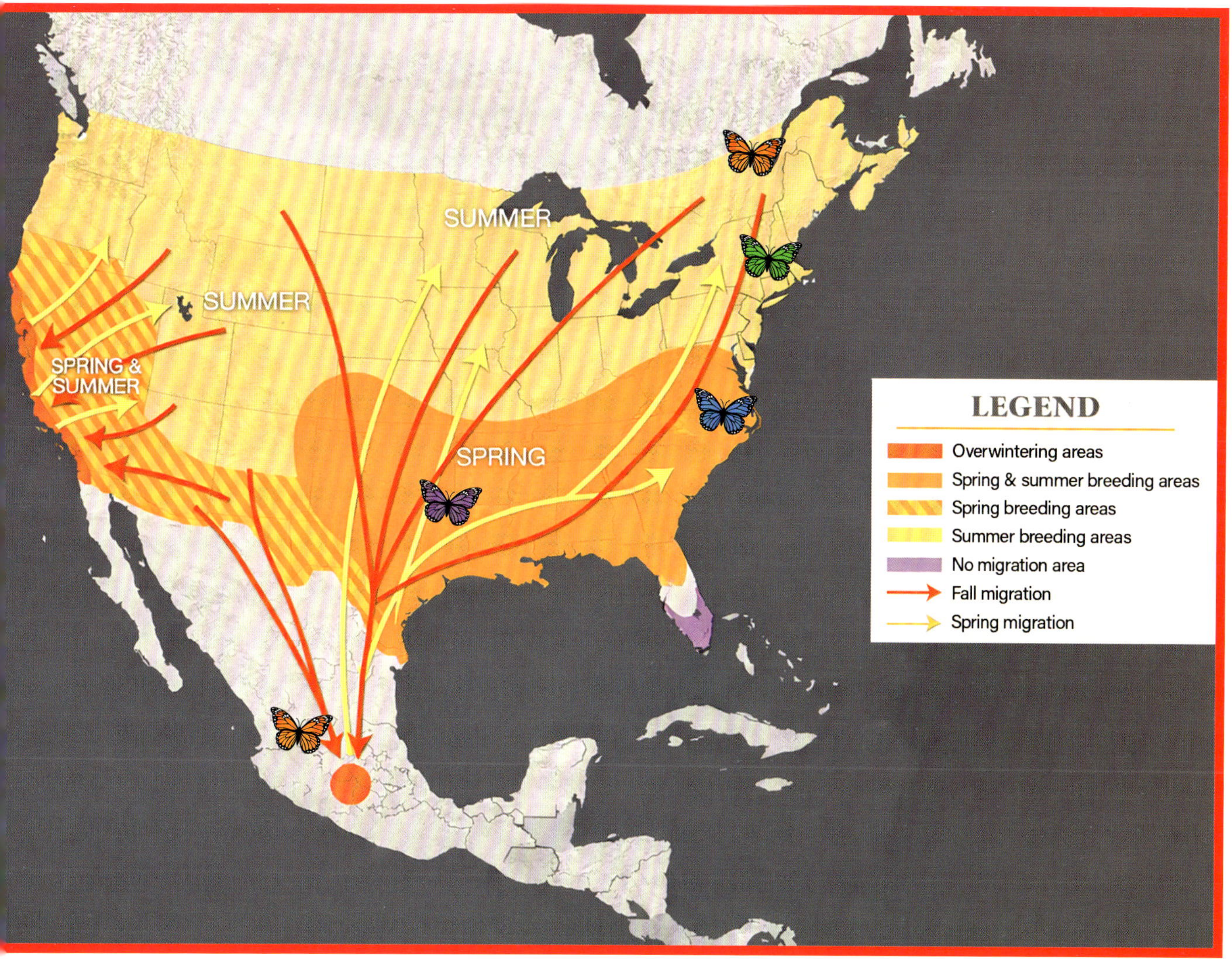
SUMMER
SUMMER
SPRING & SUMMER
SPRING
LEGEND
Overwintering areas
Spring & summer breeding areas
Spring breeding areas
Summer breeding areas
No migration area
Fall migration
Spring migration

Glossary

chrysalis (KRIS-uh-lis): a butterfly in a quiet stage of development between a caterpillar and an adult; a pupa with a hard outer covering

generation (jen-uh-RAY-shuhn): a group of butterflies that hatched and lived around the same time

instinct (IN-stingkt): behavior that is natural and not learned

magnetic field (mag-NET-ik feeld): the area around a magnet where its attractive force works; Earth's magnetic field is created by the hot, liquid metal at its center

metamorphosis (met-uh-MOR-fuh-sis): the growth process of some animals that involves a complete change at each life stage

mimic (MIM-ik): to resemble or imitate the appearance or actions of another creature

overwinter (oh-vur-WIN-tur): to survive or spend the cold winter months in a certain place

spinneret (spin-uh-RET): a special body part in spiders and caterpillars that produces silk threads

Fact Check

1. Monarch caterpillars eat ____________ leaves.

   a. fir tree b. milkweed c. grass

2. Monarchs that live a long time and spend the winter in Mexico are part of the ____________ generation.

   a. orange b. younger c. super

3. The butterfly stage that hatches out of the egg is called a ________________.

   a. caterpillar b. mimic c. chrysalis

Answers: 1. b, 2. c, 3. a

Further Reading

Baxter, Roberta. *Butterflies: Native Pollinators*. Mitchell Lane Publishers, 2020.

Lowe, Lindsey. *Butterflies and Moths*. PowerKids Press, 2019.

Unwin, Mike. *Migration: Incredible Animal Journeys*. Bloomsbury Publishing, 2019.

On the Internet

About Monarchs

https://monarchjointventure.org/monarch-biology

Learn all about monarchs, from their life cycle to migration facts to habitat needs. Check out some beautiful photos too!

Nature on the Move

https://a-z-animals.com/animals/lists/migratory-animals/

Read about monarch migrations and nine other spectacular animal migrations.

Publisher's note to educators and parents: Our editors have carefully reviewed these websites to ensure that they are suitable for students. Many websites change frequently, however, and we cannot guarantee that a site's future contents will continue to meet our high standards of quality and educational value. Be advised that students should be closely supervised whenever they access the internet.

Index

About the Authors

David and Julie Lavender love checking plants in the backyard for butterfly eggs and waiting for caterpillars to show up. They enjoy searching for chrysalises and celebrating when a butterfly emerges. The most popular butterflies in their yard are fritillaries, swallowtails, sulfurs, and zebra longwings. David and Julie especially enjoy sharing butterfly sightings with their four adult children, two sons-in-law, and three grandchildren. They are the authors of other books about animals and a picture book called *A Gingerbread House*.